CHRISTIAN DENOMINATIONS

MADE EASY

Christian Denominations Made Easy

Published by Rose Publishing
An imprint of Tyndale House Ministries
Carol Stream, Illinois
rose-publishing.com

The Made Easy series is a collection of concise, pocket-sized books that summarize key biblical teachings and provide clear, user-friendly explanations to common questions about the Christian faith. Find more Made Easy books at rose-publishing.com.

ISBN 978-1-4964-9026-1

Contributing author: Robert Bowman, Jr., PhD, President, Institute for Religious Research (IRR)

Printed in the United States of America
July 2025, 1st printing

CONTENTS

FAMILY TREE OF DENOMINATIONS

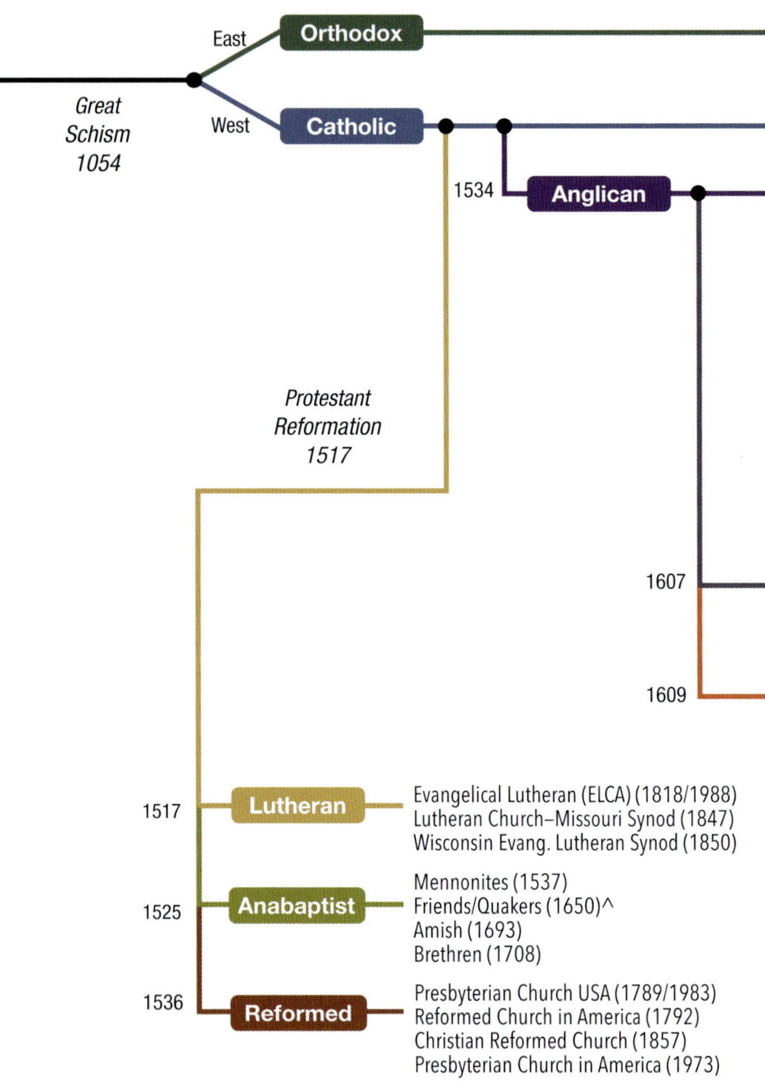

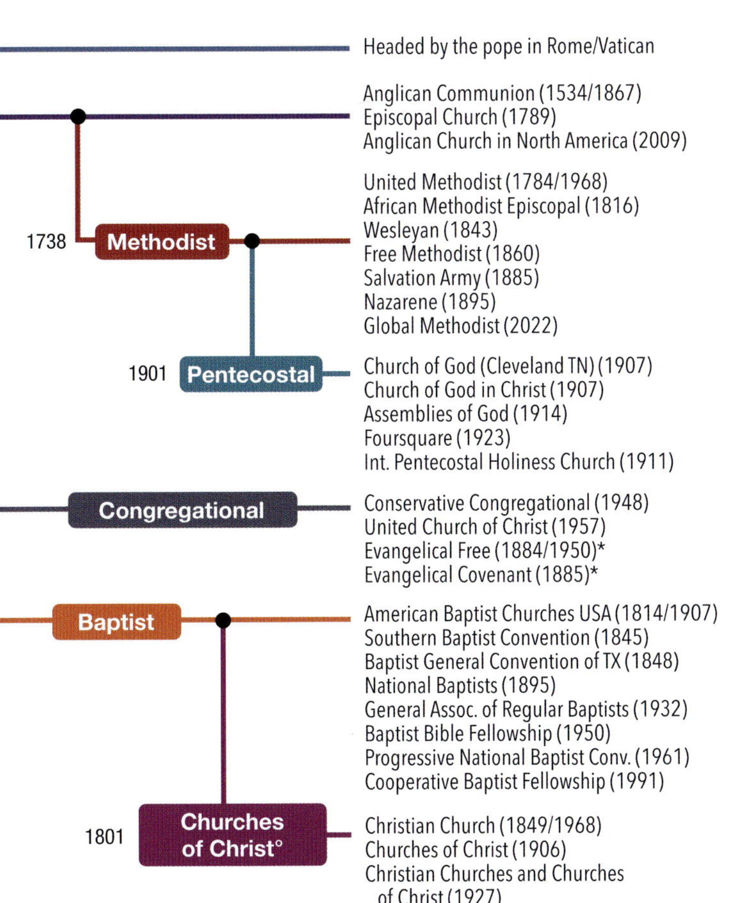

* *Historically from Lutheranism; Congregational in polity*
^ *Historically from Anglicanism; Anabaptist in practice*
° *Arose from various Protestant denominations*

WHAT ARE CHRISTIAN DENOMINATIONS?

WHAT IS A DENOMINATION?

In a strict sense, a denomination is a group of congregations and church bodies that associate together and have a formal name by which the group is known, such as "American Baptists Churches USA." In a looser sense, a denomination may be churches that share a similar heritage, as in "the Baptists." They can also be administrative organizations with affiliated congregations, as in "the Southern Baptist Convention."

Many denominations are administratively distinct groups (often in different nations or states) that share beliefs and objectives. Denominations seek to foster unity among historically related churches. They maintain consistency in doctrine and practice as they grow and establish new, like-minded congregations. Working together as a denomination, churches can pool resources to establish hospitals, universities, mission agencies, seminaries, publishing houses, and provide disaster relief.

The word *denomination* comes from the Latin *denominare*, which means "to name" or "to dub." Some denominational groups are named after their founders, such as the Mennonites, who were founded by Menno

Simons, a prominent Dutch Reformer in the 16th century. Others acquired names that reflect a distinctive teaching or spiritual practice, such as Holiness churches, which sought the complete holiness (or sanctification) of Christians. Some denominational names started as disparaging nicknames. For example, supporters of the German Reformer Martin Luther preferred to be called "evangelicals" from the Greek word *euangelion*, referring to the gospel or good news of Jesus Christ. But outsiders called them "Lutherans," and in time, Luther's adherents accepted the name. In fact, the name "Christians" was itself a nickname given to believers in Christ by pagans in Antioch (Acts 11:26).

It can be difficult nowadays to identify which denomination (if any) a local church belongs to. Many churches no longer include their denominational affiliation within their name, while still remaining part of the denomination; for example, calling their church something like "Community Church" instead of "First Baptist." (You may need to check their website or ask someone at the church to find out its denomination.) Also, many unrelated denominations have similar names. For instance, the United Church of Christ is not related to the Churches of Christ and differs from it in doctrine and practice.

Some groups do not like to be labeled as a denomination, even though in the usual sense they are a denomination. The Christian Church (Disciples of Christ) started off in the 19th century as an anti-denominational revival movement, but it eventually took on all the features of a denomination. Calvary Chapel churches, which emerged out of the Jesus Movement in the 1960s, prefer not to be classified as a denomination, but today their churches share the same name, have policies for their congregations and leaders, and so on, much like a denomination.

One of the most noticeable trends today is the rise of nondenominational churches, especially in the US. These are churches with no official ties to a denomination or direct connection to a historical denominational movement. Of the 100 fastest-growing churches in the US, nearly half (48%) are identified as nondenominational.[1]

WHAT MAKES THE DENOMINATIONS CHRISTIAN?

Christianity, simply put, is the world religion that originated with Jesus Christ. Today there are many different types of Christian churches, denominations, and movements. In the US, Christian denominations number into the hundreds, and globally into the thousands. Yet all major branches or streams of Christianity have historically agreed on some basic beliefs. So before we look at what makes the denominations in this book different, it is important to understand what makes them similar—in other words, what makes them *Christian*.

SCRIPTURE

All Christians recognize the Bible—two collections of books—as Scripture, that is, divinely revealed writings.

The Old Testament (c. 1400–400 BC) is the Christian term for a collection of texts written before the time of Jesus. This collection includes at least 39 books accepted also in Judaism as Scripture. For Catholics and Orthodox Christians, it also includes other Jewish writings, referred to as deuterocanonical writings or the deuterocanon; Protestants call them the Apocrypha.

The New Testament (c. AD 45–100) is a collection of 27 texts written by Christian apostles (spokespersons for Jesus Christ) and their associates.

These books together are called the Bible and are considered the canon (rule, authoritative list) of Scripture.

GOD

Christians are monotheists, that is, they believe in *one* God. Christians worship one God who alone created the world *ex nihilo* (out of nothing, meaning without using some eternal substance). God alone sustains and rules over all things. He is a personal being of spirit, not of matter. He has always existed and will always exist as the unchanging God. He alone has absolute power and knowledge. God is perfect in holiness, goodness, justice, and love.

Trinity symbol

Through events unfolding in the 1st century AD, Christians came to understand this one God to exist eternally in three "Persons": God the Father, his eternal Son the Lord Jesus Christ, and the Holy Spirit. Later theologians called this the Trinity.

JESUS CHRIST

Historically, Jesus of Nazareth was a Jew in the 1st century who taught about the coming of God's kingdom. During his short, three-year ministry on earth, Jesus performed miracles, healed the sick, taught his disciples, confronted the religious leaders of his day, and claimed God as his Father. He was put to death by order of the Roman governor of Judea, Pontius Pilate. Nailed to a cross, killed, and his body placed in a tomb, Jesus laid down his life. Three days later, the tomb was discovered empty, for he had risen from the dead. The resurrected Jesus appeared to family members and many disciples. He then ascended to heaven, promising to return again one day.

These events convinced many people that Jesus was truly the Messiah ("Christ") that God had promised to the Jews in the Old Testament. As they reflected on his miracles, holy life, and resurrection in the light of what he said about himself, they understood that Jesus was the divine Son of God. The Father had sent his Son from heaven to die for our salvation. The belief that Jesus was both fully divine (God by nature) and fully human is known in Christian theology as the Incarnation.

SALVATION

Christians believe that human beings are accountable to God for their behavior. All people (except Christ) are subject to eternal condemnation for the sins or offenses they commit. By coming as a human, living a sinless life, dying on the cross, and rising from the dead, Jesus Christ provided the means for people to be saved from condemnation. This salvation is a free gift of God's grace (undeserved favor) that he offers those who have genuine faith (trust) in Jesus Christ as their Savior and Lord.

THE AFTERLIFE

Believers who have died are with Christ spiritually while they await the return of Christ. At that time, all the dead will be raised, and Christ will judge all humanity. Those counted as righteous through the saving work of Christ will enjoy eternal life in immortal, glorified human bodies. They will live forever in a world free of sin and death. The Bible calls this future world "the new heavens and new earth." Christians often refer to it more simply as heaven. Those counted as wicked, who did not turn away from their sins and trust in God's mercy displayed in Christ, will be eternally separated from God (what is traditionally called hell).

THE CHURCH

The church is the community of people who have entered into relationship (both corporately and individually) with God through faith in Jesus Christ. The church in this sense includes all believers in Jesus, both living and dead, since the beginning of the church at Pentecost (Acts 2). This is sometimes called the church universal to distinguish it from the local church, which refers to specific congregations or groups of congregations (like a denomination) who meet together regularly.

SACRAMENTS/ORDINANCES

Virtually all Christian churches practice at least two rites, called either sacraments or ordinances.

The first is baptism. In the New Testament, Jesus Christ, after his resurrection, told his followers to "go and make disciples of all nations, baptizing them in the name of the Father and of the Son and of the Holy Spirit" (Matthew 28:19). Baptism is initiation with water to welcome people into the church. For many, it is a way to publicly proclaim faith in Christ. Baptism methods and requirements vary across denominations.

- Many churches will baptize infants, seeing baptism as being primarily about God initiating a person into the covenant community, based on the Old Testament model of circumcision. This includes Catholic, Orthodox, Lutheran, and Presbyterian traditions, among others.

- Other churches baptize only adults and older children who profess faith in Jesus, seeing baptism as primarily about a person's identification with the sacrificial death and resurrection of Christ. This includes most Churches of Christ, Baptist, and Pentecostal churches.

- The methods of baptism in different churches may be sprinkling, pouring, or immersion.

The second sacrament is a rite of eating bread and drinking wine or grape juice. This practice comes from the Last Supper that Jesus shared with his disciples when he broke bread and drank wine, telling his followers to "do this in remembrance of me" (Luke 22:19). Participants recall Jesus's sacrificial death on the cross, with the bread representing his body broken and the wine his blood poured out. Different denominations call this rite Communion, the Eucharist, or the Lord's Supper.

ETHICS

The Christian ethic is shaped by the liberating words of Jesus: "'Love the Lord your God with all your heart and with all your soul and with all your mind.' This is the first and greatest commandment. And the second is like it: 'Love your neighbor as yourself'" (Matthew 22:37–39). The Christian life and the church (including local bodies and denominations) are to be characterized by love of God and love of others.

In modern times, many denominations have divided over issues such as abortion, the ordination of women, same-sex marriage, and other matters of gender and sexuality.

Historically and traditionally, the major branches of Christianity have been pro-life (opposed to abortion), taught that God created humans as male and female, viewed marriage as the union of a man and a woman, regarded homosexual activity as sinful, and ordained only men to the clergy. Most denominations today have varying percentages of members and local churches who question or reject these teachings, and the mainline denominations have abandoned these traditional views.

The next chapter focuses on major denominational traditions that historically accept the Bible as the full collection of Scripture, God as the creator of all things out of nothing, and the doctrines of the Trinity and the Incarnation as taught in the historic church creeds. As such, this book does not cover groups like the Jehovah's Witnesses, the Church of Jesus Christ of Latter-day Saints (Mormons), or Unitarianism. Some specific denominations mentioned—especially mainline denominations—no longer hold to all of the following historical positions described, either officially or in practice. (See *Current Divisions and Trends* for further discussion.)

CHRISTIAN DENOMINATIONS

Christianity has three major branches: Catholic, Orthodox, and Protestant. To understand how these three branches came about, we must first go back to the beginning of the church in the 1st century AD. In the Bible, the story of how the Christian church began is told in the second chapter of the book of Acts, where the Holy Spirit descends with power upon the followers of Jesus in Jerusalem. Thousands are converted, and the good news of Jesus Christ spreads from Jerusalem to all the provinces of the Roman Empire. Early Christian congregations were centered in cities and gathered to worship in homes, rather than church buildings.

Pentecost Sunday (Acts 2)

By the start of the 2nd century, Christians had established congregations as far as Edessa (Turkey), Carthage (Tunisia), Rome (Italy), and Alexandria (Egypt). Two centuries later, churches could be found as far as Spain, Ethiopia, France, Armenia, and along northern parts of the Rhine River.

During this time, the eastern and western regions of the Roman Empire grew apart, both socially and politically. In the 5th century, the empire effectively divided into two domains: the predominantly Latin-speaking West and the predominantly Greek-speaking East.

The church became structured into five main regions, each with the bishop (or patriarch) of a major city assigned responsibility over his region: Jerusalem, Antioch, Alexandria, Rome, and Constantinople (modern-day Istanbul). Under Emperor Justinian I (who ruled AD 527–565), the five patriarchs were viewed as equal in authority; however, this view was not accepted by the Roman bishop or his churches. Over time, Rome became the most prominent center of Christianity in the West and Constantinople the center of Christianity in the East, and the two halves grew further apart.

The final split between the eastern and western churches came in the year 1054, in what has come to be called the Great Schism. The patriarch of the West and the patriarch of the East excommunicated each other. This formally separated the Catholic (western) and Orthodox (eastern) branches of Christianity.

The next major split in Christian history came in the 16th century in Europe: the Protestant Reformation.

In 1517, a German monk named Martin Luther posted his Ninety-Five Theses challenging church practices and the authority of the pope. Luther and his supporters in Germany "protested" the demand that all states under the authority of the Holy Roman Empire adhere to Catholicism. This event marks the beginning of the Protestant Reformation.

Eventually, the term *Protestant* came to encompass all denominations and churches that historically trace back to Christians who either willingly broke away from or were forced out of the Catholic Church; this includes Lutheran, Presbyterian, Congregational, and Baptist churches, among many others. (All of the denominations discussed in this chapter after the Catholic Church and Orthodox churches are generally classified as Protestant.)

CATHOLIC CHURCH

WHEN AND HOW WAS THE CHURCH FOUNDED?

Catholics consider the apostle Peter (died c. AD 66) the first bishop of Rome—the pope. Gregory the Great, who served as bishop of Rome from AD 590 until his death in 604, was arguably the first bishop who was viewed as ruling over the whole church (though not all agreed). He advanced Christian missions, liturgy, and music, something later admired by many Protestant thinkers.

St. Peter's Basilica, Vatican City

From 756 to 1870, popes were also political rulers of the papal states in central and northern Italy.

In 1929, the Lateran Treaty established part of Rome, Vatican City, as an independent city-state.

HOW MANY ADHERENTS?

- 1.3 billion worldwide, especially in Central Europe, the Philippines, Mexico, Central America, and South America
- 62 million in the US

WHAT ARE THE MAJOR DIVISIONS OR GROUPS?

Organizationally, the Catholic Church is quite unified, structured with the pope at the top; below him are cardinals, and also bishops and archbishops who oversee dioceses (districts of churches). In practice, Catholicism on the ground, so to speak, takes on more diverse forms.

Conservative Catholics accept the teachings of the Church, while liberal Catholics (the majority in the US) view both Scripture and the pope as fallible, if not unreliable guides, and they may reject the Church's teachings on abortion and human sexuality.

Some people identify as Catholic because of their ethnic background, but they practice the Catholic faith very little or not at all. They're sometimes called cultural Catholics.

Others are syncretistic, meaning that they mix Catholicism with occult-based religions, such as Santería (especially in Latin America) and the New Age Movement (especially in the US).

Small "Old Catholic" groups deny the infallibility of the pope, which the Catholic Church declared as dogma (official doctrine) at the First Vatican Council (1870).

HOW DOES THE CHURCH VIEW SCRIPTURE?

The Scriptures, which teach without error the truth needed for salvation, must be interpreted within Church Tradition. The canon consists of 46 Old Testament books, including 7 deuterocanonical books (the Apocrypha), and 27 New Testament books.

HOW DOES THE CHURCH VIEW GOD AND SALVATION?

The Catholic Church accepts the doctrines of the Trinity and the Incarnation as taught in the creeds. The Church teaches that Christ died as a sacrifice for people's sins. By grace, God infuses a gift of faith in Christ in those who are baptized, which they maintain as they mature by doing works of love and receiving the sacraments.

WHAT DOES THE CHURCH BELIEVE HAPPENS AFTER DEATH?

The souls of the faithful go to heaven either immediately or, if imperfectly purified in this life, after purgatory. Purgatory is a temporary state of both punishment and purification before admission into heaven. The wicked immediately go to eternal punishment in hell.

HOW IS THE CHURCH VIEWED?

The church is the Mystical Body of Christ, established by Christ and led by its earthly head, the pope, who may infallibly pronounce dogma (doctrines all members must believe) when he speaks *ex cathedra* ("from the chair")—that is, from the position Catholics believe was originally held by Peter. It is united (one) in a sacred (holy) worldwide (catholic) community through the succession of bishops whose ordination goes back to the apostles (apostolic). Christians not in the Catholic Church are considered "separated brethren."

WHAT ABOUT THE SACRAMENTS?

Baptism removes original sin in infants and converts.

The Eucharist is the central event in the service called the Mass, which follows a liturgy—a standardized order and form with a script spoken by both priest and laity. In the Eucharist, the substances (not the properties) of bread and wine are changed into Jesus's body and blood (transubstantiation).

Confession, Confirmation, Holy Matrimony, Holy Orders (ordinations), and Anointing of the Sick (last rites) are also sacraments.

WHAT OTHER THINGS SHOULD WE KNOW?

Anyone in heaven is considered a saint (holy one), but the Catholic Church canonizes (formally recognizes) heroic and auspiciously virtuous members (for example, martyrs) who have died as appropriate objects of devotion, whom Catholics may ask to intercede for them. By far the most important, popular saint in Catholicism is Mary, the mother of Jesus.

The Church teaches that Mary was conceived by her mother immaculately (free of original sin), remained a virgin perpetually, and was assumed bodily into heaven without dying. She is the Mother of the Church and an object of veneration (honor that stops short of worship). Much of this devotion is associated with reported apparitions of Mary, especially in Mexico City (1531), Lourdes, France (1858), and Fatima, Portugal (1917).

Priests and those in higher positions must be celibate (unmarried) men.

For most of its history, the Church taught that capital punishment could be legitimate, but in 2018, under Pope Francis, the Church clearly stated its opposition to the practice.

FAMOUS CATHOLICS

- Pope Leo the Great (in office 440–461), who helped define the doctrine of the deity and humanity of Christ set forth at the Council of Chalcedon (451)
- St. Thomas Aquinas (1225–1274), the most influential Catholic theologian of the past thousand years

- St. Catherine of Siena (1347–1380) and St. Teresa of Avila (1515–1582), both influential Catholic mystics
- Sir Thomas More (1478–1535), an English statesman who was executed for refusing to recognize King Henry VIII as the head of the Church of England
- St. Junipero Serra (1713–1784), a Franciscan priest who founded the missions that became Los Angeles, San Francisco, and San Diego
- Pope Pius IX (in office 1846–1878), the last pope to rule the Papal States, who set forth the dogmas of the Immaculate Conception (Mary's being conceived in her mother's womb without sin) and papal infallibility, and convened the First Vatican Council (1868–1870) to support those dogmas
- J. R. R. Tolkien (1892–1973), author of *The Lord of the Rings*
- Mother Teresa (1910–1997), an Albanian nun who served the poor in Calcutta, India, and received the Nobel Peace Prize in 1979 for her humanitarian work; in 2016, she was canonized as St. Teresa of Calcutta.
- Pope John Paul II (in office 1978–2005), an influential pope who played a role in the fall of Communism; he was also the first non-Italian pope since 1523 and the third longest-serving pope.
- US presidents: John F. Kennedy and Joseph R. Biden Jr.

MONASTICISM

Monasticism developed initially within eastern Christianity around the 3rd and 4th centuries (if not earlier), and it was quickly adopted by the western churches as well.

In the early period of Christianity, some Christians withdrew to the desert to live as hermits or in small communities (monasteries). They lived devout lives of prayer, meditation, fasting, celibacy, and Scripture reading and memorization. In the centuries that followed, monasteries reached outward and flourished as centers of education and medical care for the poor. Leading monks and nuns spurred the formation of distinct religious orders, such as St. Francis of Assisi (1182–1226) whose example led to the Franciscan order, known for their work among the poor; and St. Ignatius of Loyola (1491–1556) who founded the Society of Jesus (Jesuits), known for their work in education and foreign missions.

Today, there are hundreds of orders in the Catholic Church. Some of the most well-known orders include:

- for men: Dominican, Franciscan, Jesuit, and Benedictine;

- for women: Benedictine, Discalced Carmelites, Missionaries of Charity (Mother Theresa's order), and The Poor Clares.

ORTHODOX CHURCHES

WHEN AND HOW WERE THEY FOUNDED?

Orthodox churches formed in the Greek-speaking cultures in the East (Byzantium/Constantinople), rather than the Latin-speaking West (Rome).

In the 5th century, the Roman Empire divided politically into East and West. The church in Europe, the Middle East, and Northern Africa was structured into five main regions, each with the bishop (or patriarch) of a major city overseeing his region—including the cities of Rome and Constantinople.

Eventually, in 1054, the Eastern Church and Western Church formally separated in the Great Schism. Hence, the name Eastern Orthodox is commonly used to refer to the churches not part of the Catholic West.

People's Salvation Cathedral, Bucharest, Romania

HOW MANY ADHERENTS?

- 220 million worldwide
- 1.2 million in the US, a third of which are part of the Greek Orthodox Church

WHAT ARE THEIR MAJOR DIVISIONS OR GROUPS?

The Orthodox Church is organized by nations (Greek, Coptic, Russian, Armenian, etc.), each also with churches representing people of those ethnicities in other countries.

HOW DO THEY VIEW SCRIPTURE?

Scripture, without error in matters of faith, is to be interpreted by Sacred Tradition, especially the seven Ecumenical Councils (AD 325–787). The canon consists of 49 Old Testament books (including the Catholic deuterocanonical books, plus three more books and short additions to two others) and 27 New Testament books.

HOW DO THEY VIEW GOD AND SALVATION?

The Orthodox Church accepts the doctrines of the Trinity and the Incarnation as taught in the creeds. In Christ, God became human so that humans might be deified (*theosis*), having the energy of God's life in them. Through baptism and church participation, people receive the benefits of Christ's death and resurrection as they persevere (follow a path of spiritual ascent toward mystical union with God).

WHAT DO THEY BELIEVE HAPPENS AFTER DEATH?

The souls of the faithful are purified (a process of growth, not punishment), then get a foretaste of eternal blessing in heaven. The wicked get a foretaste of eternal torment in hell.

HOW DO THEY VIEW THE CHURCH?

The church is the Body of Christ in unbroken historical connection to the apostles, changelessly maintaining the faith of the undivided church as expressed in the Creeds. It is one, holy, catholic, and apostolic. Each national church has bishops under the leadership of Patriarchs. The Patriarch of Constantinople has primacy of honor.

WHAT ABOUT THE SACRAMENTS?

Baptism initiates God's life in infants and converts, and it is practiced by immersion.

In the Eucharist, the bread and wine are changed into Jesus's body and blood—a Mystery left unexplained.

Chrismation (receiving of the seal of the Holy Spirit through anointing with oil), Confession, Marriage, Holy Orders, and Anointing of the Sick are also sacraments—crucial aids in the progress of believers in their spiritual ascent.

WHAT OTHER THINGS SHOULD WE KNOW?

Orthodox Christians believe that Mary was cleansed of sin when Gabriel appeared to her, remained a virgin perpetually, and (in tradition, not dogma) was assumed bodily into heaven.

The most important saints are Mary and John the Baptist; others include Old Testament prophets, New Testament apostles, and martyrs. Orthodox Christians seek intercession with God by Mary and the saints on their behalf.

Icons are pictures of Christ or saints. Relics are bones or objects belonging to or associated with specific saints (generally kept in churches named for them). Both icons and relics are objects through which the saints are venerated and through which Christ is worshiped.

Iconostasis (a wall of icons) in an Orthodox church

Bishops are to be celibate men, but priests may be married men.

Monks and nuns live celibate lives in separate communities (monasteries), usually away from cities, devoting their days to the study of Scripture, liturgical services, fasting, and especially prayer.

FAMOUS ORTHODOX CHRISTIANS

- St. Gregory Palamas (c. 1296–1359), an early, influential Orthodox theologian who formulated the distinction between God's essence (or nature, which humans cannot have) and his energies (such as grace, which God can impart to humans); this distinction became basic to the Orthodox doctrine of *theosis*—humans can become "divine" by having God's energies.

- Fyodor Dostoevsky (1821–1881), the Russian Orthodox author of *The Brothers Karamazov*
- Igor Stravinsky (1882–1971), a Russian Orthodox composer and conductor best known for his ballets
- Kallistos Ware (1934–2022), who as a young man converted from Anglicanism to Orthodoxy and became the most influential modern theologian explaining Orthodoxy to the English-speaking world
- St. Porphyrios (1906–1991), a Greek Orthodox monk revered for his spiritual discernment, humility, and piety
- Seraphim Rose (1934–1982), a convert to Orthodoxy who became a monk and spread Orthodox teachings in North America
- Actors Tom Hanks, Rita Wilson, and Tina Fey

LUTHERAN CHURCHES

WHEN AND HOW WERE THEY FOUNDED?

Martin Luther was an Augustinian monk in the Catholic Church. Luther's posting of his Ninety-Five Theses—reportedly on a church door in Wittenberg, Germany, on October 31, 1517—typically marks the beginning of the Protestant Reformation. His document criticized various Catholic practices of his day, most famously the sale of indulgences, which were supposed reductions in the time someone would need to spend in purgatory.

Martin Luther (1483–1546)

About two years later, Luther had a personal "breakthrough." As he was teaching the Bible, he realized that "the righteousness of God" described in Paul's epistle to the Romans was God's gift of righteousness received by faith alone. Luther actively sought the reformation of the church, not to divide it. Nevertheless, in 1521, Pope Leo X excommunicated him. Over the following years, Luther worked with others to establish a gospel-based church.

The Augsburg Confession (1530), written by theologian Philip Melanchthon, became the first formal Lutheran confession.

HOW MANY ADHERENTS?

- 80 million worldwide, with half in central and northern Europe
- 6.5 million in the US

WHAT ARE THEIR MAJOR DIVISIONS OR GROUPS?

The Church of Sweden is Evangelical Lutheran, with an estimated 5.5 million members, roughly half the population of Sweden. Until 2000, Lutheranism had been the official religion of Sweden.

Main Lutheran US bodies:

- The Evangelical Lutheran Church in America (ELCA) (1818/1988), a mainline denomination
- The Lutheran Church—Missouri Synod (LCMS) (1847) and the Wisconsin Evangelical Lutheran Synod (WELS) (1850), both conservative denominations
- There are also a dozen or more smaller Lutheran denominations.

HOW DO THEY VIEW SCRIPTURE?

Scripture alone is the authoritative witness to the gospel (some parts more directly or fully than others). The Protestant canon of 39 Old Testament books and 27 New Testament books is accepted. Conservatives view Scripture as inerrant (without error).

HOW DO THEY VIEW GOD AND SALVATION?

The doctrines of the Trinity and the Incarnation as taught in the creeds are accepted. Lutherans believe that people are saved by grace alone when God justifies them (imputes his gift of righteousness) through faith alone (*sola fide*) in Christ who died for their sins. Justification by faith alone is the heart of the gospel. Good works are the inevitable result of true faith but not the basis of right standing before God. Conservative Lutherans generally affirm that God chooses who will be saved before they believe (predestination).

WHAT DO THEY BELIEVE HAPPENS AFTER DEATH?

The souls of believers go immediately to be with Christ, and at Christ's return, their bodies are raised to immortal, eternal life. The wicked begin suffering immediately in hell.

HOW DO THEY VIEW THE CHURCH?

The church is the congregation of believers (though mixed with the lost) in which the gospel is preached and sacraments are rightly administered.

Believers are priests in that they have direct access to God ("priesthood of all believers"). All ministers are pastors, and some serve as bishops. Churches are governed primarily at a local level, with congregations electing representatives who together form a synod.

Historically, Lutherans reject apostolic succession—the teaching that bishops represent an uninterrupted line which traces back to the New Testament apostles.

WHAT ABOUT THE SACRAMENTS?

Baptism is necessary for salvation; in it, both infants and adult converts are given God's grace.

The Lord's Supper remains truly bread and wine but also becomes truly Jesus's body and blood. This is sometimes called consubstantiation, though most Lutherans prefer the the term sacramental union.

WHAT OTHER THINGS SHOULD WE KNOW?

Lutheran liturgy revised the Catholic liturgy to put more emphasis on preaching of the Word.

The ELCA, a mainline denomination, ordains women and permits congregations to perform same-sex marriage ceremonies, unlike conservative denominations, such as the LCMS and the WELS. Other differences between the ELCA and conservative denominations include views about the authority and inerrancy of Scripture, with conservatives taking the traditional view.

FAMOUS LUTHERANS

- Johannes Kepler (1571–1630), who developed the laws of planetary motion and argued that God had designed the world
- Philipp Spener (1635–1705), the theologian who originated pietism, a Protestant movement that emphasized living a devotional life
- Johann Sebastian Bach (1685–1750), the composer of the Brandenberg Concertos and famous organ and choral music
- George Frideric Handel (1685–1759), a composer in Germany, Italy, and England, best known for his "Hallelujah Chorus" in *Messiah*
- Søren Kierkegaard (1813–1855), a Danish philosopher who challenged the cultural Christianity of Lutheranism in Denmark
- Dietrich Bonhoeffer (1906–1945), a German pastor and theologian who stood against Nazi co-opting of the church and who was executed in the final days of World War II

ANABAPTIST CHURCHES

WHEN AND HOW WERE THEY FOUNDED?

In 1525, Protestants in Zurich, Switzerland, began practicing believer's baptism rather than infant baptism. They were nicknamed Anabaptists, which means "baptizing again"—a term they initially rejected because they denied that infant baptism was ever a valid baptism in the first place. Anabaptism was a grass-roots movement during the Protestant Reformation. They were seen as the radicals; they advocated for greater separation of church and state, and many Anabaptist groups opposed the leading Reformers of their day.

In 1527, the Schleitheim Confession (named for its city of origin), probably written by Michael Sattler (who was soon thereafter martyred), set forth seven principles of Anabaptism.

Various groups grew out from the Anabaptist movement:

- **Moravians:** Before the Protestant Reformation began, a Czech Catholic priest named Jan Hus (c. 1370–1415) was burned at the stake for advocating sweeping reforms. He is seen as a key pre-Protestant figure anticipating the Anabaptist movement. Moravians trace their origins to Jan Hus, and so Moravian churches are not technically Anabaptist but are a kindred group.

- **Mennonites:** In 1537, Dutch Reformer Menno Simons began teaching a pacifist form of Anabaptism. His followers became known as Mennonites.

Menno Simons (1496–1561)

- **Quakers:** In England in the 17th century, Margaret Fell and George Fox founded the Religious Society of Friends, nicknamed Quakers. This group is not Anabaptist per se but has historically been included among the peace churches. In 1681, William Penn, a member of the Friends, established Pennsylvania as a haven of religious liberty. Groups such as the Mennonites who had faced persecution in their home countries soon migrated to Pennsylvania.

- **Amish:** Swiss minister Jakob Ammann (c. 1644–1730) led a Mennonite group (nicknamed Amish after his last name) that practiced a strict church discipline called "shunning."

- **Brethren:** Also called the German Baptists, the Brethren were founded by Alexander Mack in Germany in 1708. Both the Brethren and the Amish migrated to Pennsylvania.

HOW MANY ADHERENTS?

- 2 million or more worldwide
- 800,000 in the US

WHAT ARE THEIR MAJOR DIVISIONS OR GROUPS?

The Mennonite Church (1725) and the Church of the Brethren (1708) are the largest Anabaptist bodies.

There are close to a million Moravians, most of them in Africa, and roughly 400,000 Quakers, about half in Africa.

In 2013, the Moravians, Mennonites, and Friends united as one confessional family for purposes of representation in the World Council of Churches.

HOW DO THEY VIEW SCRIPTURE?

Most view Scripture as the inspired means for following Jesus, but not as infallible. Scripture is the written Word pointing to Jesus, the living Word. The Protestant canon is accepted.

HOW DO THEY VIEW GOD AND SALVATION?

Most affirm the Trinity but are noncreedal (do not require adherence to church creeds). Jesus is viewed as a man in whom God's will was revealed by his life of service and by his suffering and death. His deity, virgin birth, and resurrection are traditionally affirmed. Through faith in Jesus, believers experience peace with God, moving them to follow Jesus's example by living as peacemakers in the world. How believers live is emphasized over having correct doctrine.

WHAT DO THEY BELIEVE HAPPENS AFTER DEATH?

There is no official view of what happens immediately after death. The traditional view is that at Christ's return, God's people will be raised to eternal life and the unrepentant will be forever separated from God.

HOW DO THEY VIEW THE CHURCH?

The church is the body of Christ, the society of Christ's followers, marked by holiness, love, service, a simple lifestyle, and peacemaking.

Quaker Meeting House (1782), Adams, Massachusetts

No one system of church government is recognized. Church leaders (who function mostly locally) are to be characterized by humble service. All believers are to be considered equal in the church.

Members who repeatedly commit sin after being warned twice should be excommunicated This policy is an example of a broader principle of Christians keeping themselves separate from evil.

WHAT ABOUT THE SACRAMENTS?

Baptism is for believers only, a sign of commitment to follow Jesus.

The Lord's Supper is a memorial of his death and is only for those baptized as believers.

WHAT OTHER THINGS SHOULD WE KNOW?

They emphasize equality of believers and the autonomy of congregations.

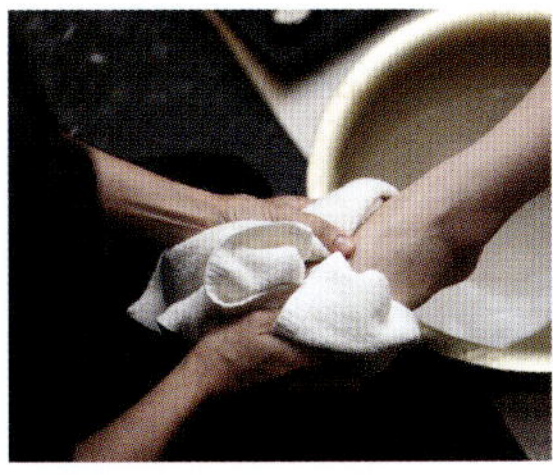

Some churches practice foot washing, imitating Jesus's act of humility, service, and love when he washed his disciples' feet at the Last Supper (John 13:1–17).

Most groups are "peace churches," teaching nonresistance and pacifism, the view that participation in war is wrong. Many also believe that Christians should not hold government office or take oaths.

Doctrine is deemphasized, and liberal views prevail in some church bodies. Views on the ordination of women and same-sex marriage vary widely among the different church bodies.

Friends (Quaker) churches do not practice baptism or Communion.

FAMOUS MEMBERS OF ANABAPTIST CHURCHES

- Joan Baez, a popular folk musician, who drew her themes of peace and social justice in the 1960s and 70s from her Quaker faith
- Richard J. Foster, a Quaker pastor and writer best known for his book *Celebration of Discipline* (1978), which reintroduced spiritual disciplines to the broader Christian community
- Ronald J. Sider (1939–2022), a Mennonite and Brethren scholar and author of *Rich Christians in an Age of Hunger* who advocated for social justice
- Andy Griffith (1926–2012), a popular TV actor and a Moravian
- US presidents: Herbert Hoover and Richard Nixon were both raised as Quakers but were largely inactive as adults.

ANGLICAN AND EPISCOPAL CHURCHES

WHEN AND HOW WERE THEY FOUNDED?

In 1534, Parliament declared King Henry VIII to be the head of the Church in England (Anglican Church). In doing so, they rejected the pope as the head of the church and made the Church of England independent of the Catholic Church. Following the short reign of Queen Mary (1553–1558), who tried to reestablish Catholicism as England's official religion, the Act of Supremacy restored church authority under the Crown, and Queen Elizabeth I solidified the Church of England as Protestant.

Canterbury Cathedral, England

In 1611, Anglican scholars produced the King James Version, a Bible translation that became the most popular English version for the next three centuries.

In 1789, the Episcopal Church was formed by American Anglicans seeking to distance themselves from England after the Revolutionary War.

HOW MANY ADHERENTS?

- 85 million worldwide, with about half in Africa
- 1.75 million in the US

WHAT ARE THEIR MAJOR DIVISIONS OR GROUPS?

Anglican Communion (1867) is a worldwide union of national and provincial churches.

The largest US body is the Episcopal Church (1789), a mainline denomination.

In 2009, US conservatives formed the Anglican Church in North America (ACNA).

HOW DO THEY VIEW SCRIPTURE?

Scripture contains the truth necessary for salvation and is the primary norm for faith but must be interpreted in light of tradition and reason. The Protestant canon is accepted. The Apocrypha is respected but not viewed as Scripture.

HOW DO THEY VIEW GOD AND SALVATION?

The doctrines of the Trinity and the Incarnation as taught in the creeds are accepted. Christ suffered and died as an offering for sin, freeing people from sin and reconciling them to God. People share in Christ's victory when infants and converts are baptized and become living members of the church, believing in him and keeping his commandments.

WHAT DO THEY BELIEVE HAPPENS AFTER DEATH?

The souls of the faithful are purified to enjoy full communion with God. At Christ's return, they are raised to fullness of eternal life in heaven. Those who reject God face eternal death.

HOW DO THEY VIEW THE CHURCH?

The church is the Body of Christ. Its unity is based on faithfulness to apostolic teaching and the apostolic succession of bishops. It is one, holy, catholic (universal), and apostolic.

Anglican church service in Soroti, Uganda

Anglicans and Episcopalians hold to an "episcopal" form of church government, meaning that the church is led by bishops (*episkopoi*). An archbishop has oversight of bishops in a particular region, and in turn each bishop oversees ministers and their local congregations.

The unity of the worldwide Anglican Communion is traditionally represented by the archbishop of Canterbury. This tradition is now in question as Anglicanism has grown outside of England, especially in Africa, and as Anglicanism in England and North America has become increasingly liberal. This has led to conservative branches separating off.

WHAT ABOUT THE SACRAMENTS?

The sacraments are outward and visible signs of an inward and spiritual grace.

Infants and converts are made part of the church in baptism.

In Communion, Christ's body and blood are really present (the "real spiritual presence").

The other five Catholic sacraments are accepted but with lesser authority and status.

WHAT OTHER THINGS SHOULD WE KNOW?

Anglicans consider their church as taking a "middle way" (*via media*) between Catholicism and Protestantism. Members are free to accept or reject Catholic doctrines of Mary.

The *Book of Common Prayer*, which includes a modified version of Catholic liturgy, represents the norm for Anglican piety.

Priests and bishops may be married. Both the Episcopal Church and the majority of ACNA churches ordain women. The Episcopal Church affirms same-sex marriages; the ACNA does not permit same-sex marriages.

FAMOUS ANGLICANS AND EPISCOPALIANS

- Thomas Cranmer (1489–1556) was the Archbishop of Canterbury who supported the recognition of King Henry VIII as the head of the Church of England. Cranmer compiled the first *Book of Common Prayer*. He was later burned at the stake by order of the Catholic queen, Mary.

- John Newton (1725–1807) was a former slave ship captain who converted to Christianity and became an abolitionist. He wrote the hymn "Amazing Grace." Among the many people he influenced was fellow-Anglican William Wilberforce (1759–1833), who spearheaded the effort in Parliament to abolish the slave trade throughout the British Empire.

- Samuel Ajayi Crowther (c. 1807–1891), an Anglican bishop and missionary and former slave from Yoruba (modern-day Nigeria) who translated parts of the New Testament into his native language of Yoruba

- Dorothy L. Sayers (1893–1957), an English detective writer and scholar

- C. S. Lewis (1898–1963), the author of *The Chronicles of Narnia* and *Mere Christianity*

- John R. W. Stott (1921–2011), an Anglican pastor and leading figure in evangelicalism throughout the world, and also chaplain to Queen Elizabeth II (who was also outspoken about her Christian faith)
- Charlton Heston (1923–2008), an Episcopalian, famous for his roles in blockbuster biblical films *The Ten Commandments* (produced and directed by Cecil B. DeMille, another devout Episcopalian) and *Ben-Hur*
- J. I. Packer (1926–2020), an Anglican theologian and premier evangelical scholar of the 20th century
- Desmond Tutu (1931–2021), an Anglican cleric and theologian known for drawing international attention to the evils of apartheid (policy of racial segregation) in South Africa; he was awarded the Nobel Peace Prize in 1984.
- US presidents who were Episcopalians: George Washington, James Madison, James Monroe, William Henry Harrison, John Tyler, Zachary Taylor, Franklin Pierce, Chester Arthur, Franklin D. Roosevelt, Gerald Ford, and George H. W. Bush

REFORMED AND PRESBYTERIAN CHURCHES

WHEN AND HOW WERE THEY FOUNDED?

The Reformed branch of Protestantism began with John Calvin, a French Reformer in Geneva, Switzerland, often considered to be the most influential theologian of the Reformation. His work *Institutes of the Christian Religion* (1536) is a classic of Reformed theology. Calvin's teachings emphasize the sovereignty of God over the world and over human salvation, especially with the doctrines of predestination and perseverance of the saints (believers).

John Calvin (1509–1564)

Calvin's reform movement spread throughout Europe and resulted in formative confessional documents, such as the Belgic Confession (1561) and the Heidelberg Catechism (1563).

John Knox, a Scottish preacher and student of Calvin, steered the Reformation in Scotland. In 1560, he led a group of writers to produce the Scots Confession, an early statement of Presbyterian theology. The Westminster Confession of Faith and the other Westminster Standards (1643–1649) were drawn up by over a hundred theologians and members of the English

Parliament; these define Reformed doctrine for many Presbyterian churches today.

HOW MANY ADHERENTS?

- 70–80 million worldwide
- 2 million in the US

WHAT ARE THEIR MAJOR DIVISIONS OR GROUPS?

The Presbyterian Church (USA), or PCUSA, a mainline church (1789), took its present form through a merger in 1983.

The conservative Presbyterian Church in America (PCA) formed in 1973 to avoid the PCUSA merger.

First Presbyterian Church of Hollywood

The Reformed Church in America (RCA) was founded in 1628 by a handful of Dutch immigrants in New York ("New Amsterdam"). Over time, the church gained its independence from the church in Holland, ratified its constitution (1792), and adopted its present name (1867).

The Christian Reformed Church (CRC) (1857) was founded by Dutch immigrants seceding from the RCA, a mainline and more liberal denomination.

HOW DO THEY VIEW SCRIPTURE?

Scripture is inspired and infallible, the sole, final rule of faith. The Protestant canon is accepted.

HOW DO THEY VIEW GOD AND SALVATION?

The doctrines of the Trinity and the Incarnation as taught in the creeds are accepted. People are saved by grace alone when God imputes his gift of righteousness through faith alone (*sola fide*) in Christ, who died for their sins. Good works are the inevitable result of true faith but in no way the basis of right standing before God.

WHAT DO THEY BELIEVE HAPPENS AFTER DEATH?

The souls of believers go immediately to be with Christ. At Christ's return, their bodies are raised to immortal, eternal life. The wicked begin suffering immediately in hell.

HOW DO THEY VIEW THE CHURCH?

The church is the body of Christ, including all whom God has chosen as his people, represented by the visible church, composed of churches that vary in purity and corruption. Christ alone is the head of the church. Congregations choose elders (presbyters) to govern them. Regional groups of elders (presbyteries) meet in denomination-wide assemblies.

WHAT ABOUT THE SACRAMENTS?

Baptism is not necessary for salvation but is a sign of the new covenant of grace for adults and infants.

In the Lord's Supper, Christ's body and blood are spiritually present to believers.

WHAT OTHER THINGS SHOULD WE KNOW?

Calvinists and others in the Reformed tradition emphasize the five *solas*: (1) on the authority of Scripture alone, (2) by grace alone, (3) through faith alone, (4) in Christ alone, and (5) to the glory of God alone.

FAMOUS PRESBYTERIANS AND REFORMED MEMBERS

- Abraham Kuyper (1837–1920), a leading Dutch Calvinist intellectual, founder of the Free University of Amsterdam, and prime minister of the Netherlands

- Henrietta Mears (1890–1963), a Presbyterian educator who inspired excellence in curricula and robust evangelism through the Sunday school movement

- D. James Kennedy (1930–2007), a Presbyterian pastor, author, and radio and television broadcaster, and the creator of the popular lay training program Evangelism Explosion

- R. C. Sproul (1939–2017), a Presbyterian professor, author, and founder of Ligonier Ministries, widely regarded as an influential advocate for Calvinist theology

- James ("Jimmy") Stewart (1908–1997), an actor and notably devout, lifelong Presbyterian

- Katherine Johnson (1918–2020), a NASA scientist and mathematician who pioneered the use of computers in space exploration and the moon landing, and a devout and active Presbyterian

- Fred Rogers ("Mister Rogers") (1928–2003), the popular TV host of *Mister Roger's Neighborhood,* and also an ordained Presbyterian minister

- US presidents: Andrew Jackson (Presbyterian after he left office), Martin Van Buren (Dutch Reformed), James Buchanan (Presbyterian), Grover Cleveland (Presbyterian), Benjamin Harrison (Presbyterian), Theodore Roosevelt (Presbyterian with Dutch Reformed roots), Woodrow Wilson (theologically liberal Presbyterian), Dwight D. Eisenhower (raised Brethren and baptized Presbyterian while in office), and Ronald Reagan (raised in the Disciples of Christ but from 1963 was Presbyterian)

CONGREGATIONAL CHURCHES

WHEN AND HOW WERE THEY FOUNDED?

In the early 17th century, English Puritans who sought to purify the Church of England said that each church congregation should govern itself without the permission or oversight of the bishops or priests—hence, "congregationalism." This stance quickly forced many into exile in Holland. In 1620, these separatists in Holland sailed on the Mayflower to Plymouth, Massachusetts. In 1630, other Puritans settled in the Massachusetts Bay Colony, also seeking a new land in which to practice their religion freely.

Park Street Congregational Church, Boston, Massachusetts

The Savoy Declaration (1658), an English Puritan revision of the Westminster Confession of Faith, set forth Congregational theology.

Similar "free churches" arose in the US in the 1880s among Swedes who had separated from the Lutheran Church and had immigrated to America. While these churches historically grew out of Lutheranism, they were congregational in practice.

HOW MANY ADHERENTS?

- 500,000 worldwide
- 400,000 in the US

WHAT ARE THEIR MAJOR DIVISIONS OR GROUPS?

Congregationalists fractured in the 18th and 19th centuries. Most eventually became liberal (denying the reliability of Scripture) and Unitarian (denying the Trinity); these churches generally do not call themselves Congregational.

Signing of the Savoy Declaration (1658)

The main traditional body of Puritan origins today is the (quite small) Conservative Congregational Christian Conference (1948).

The Evangelical Free Church of America (1884/1950) and the Evangelical Covenant Church (1885) are conservative groups from the Swedish free church movement.

The United Church of Christ (1957), a liberal and mainline denomination, traces its origins in part to Congregationalism. It also has roots in the Reformed tradition and the Restoration Movement.

HOW DO THEY VIEW SCRIPTURE?

The conservative bodies view Scripture as the inerrant word of God, and the Protestant canon is accepted.

HOW DO THEY VIEW GOD AND SALVATION?

The doctrines of the Trinity and the Incarnation, generally in line with the historic church creeds, are accepted, though these churches typically make little use of those creeds. People are saved by grace alone when God makes them right with him through faith alone in Christ, who died for their sins. Good works are the result of true faith but in no way the basis of right standing before God.

WHAT DO THEY BELIEVE HAPPENS AFTER DEATH?

The souls of believers go immediately to be with Christ, and at Christ's return, their bodies are raised to immortality. The wicked will suffer eternal punishment in hell.

HOW DO THEY VIEW THE CHURCH?

The church is the people of God gathered in Christ's name. Each local church is self-governing and chooses its own ministers.

WHAT ABOUT THE SACRAMENTS?

The sacraments are symbols of spiritual realities. Congregations may practice infant baptism and/or believer's baptism. The Lord's Supper is practiced as a memorial of Christ's death and resurrection.

WHAT OTHER THINGS SHOULD WE KNOW?

The practice of congregationalism is based on the priesthood of all believers, and, by extension, their equality before God and in the church (1 Peter 2:5–9).

Congregationalists founded many schools, including Harvard (1636), Yale (1701), and Dartmouth (1769).

FAMOUS CONGREGATIONALISTS

- John Bunyan (1628–1688), an English Puritan pastor who wrote *The Pilgrim's Progress*
- Jonathan Edwards (1703–1758), a leading minister in the First Great Awakening in New England
- Noah Webster (1758–1843), a foundational figure in American education and the author of not only the original Webster's Dictionary but also a revision of the King James Version of the Bible
- Laura Ingalls Wilder (1867–1957), the author of *Little House on the Prairie*
- Craig Groeschel, the pastor and founder of Life.Church, an Evangelical Covenant Church and the largest megachurch in the US
- US presidents: Calvin Coolidge (Congregational); Barack Obama was a longtime member of the United Church of Christ until resigning his membership in 2008 before his election.

BAPTIST CHURCHES

WHEN AND HOW WERE THEY FOUNDED?

In 1609, John Smyth, Thomas Helwys, and other English Puritans formed the first Baptist church in Amsterdam. They were called Baptists because they baptized only professing believers. (Though the Baptists rejected infant baptism like the Anabaptists, they originated independently of the Anabaptist movement.) A few years later, Helwys returned to his homeland, and in London, he founded the first Baptist church in England. Baptists resisted state control of the church in England and began as independent congregations.

First Baptist Church in America, Providence, Rhode Island

In 1638, the first Baptist church in America was established in Providence, Rhode Island, by Roger Williams, a Puritan who had been banished from the Massachusetts Bay Colony, largely for his advocacy of separation of church and state.

HOW MANY ADHERENTS?

- 100 million worldwide (including families)
- 25–30 million in the US

WHAT ARE THEIR MAJOR DIVISIONS OR GROUPS?

American Baptist Churches USA (1814/1907), a mainline denomination

The conservative Southern Baptist Convention (SBC) (1845) is by far the largest US Protestant denomination (13 million). Of the 100 largest churches in the US, 18 are in the SBC.[2]

Baptist General Convention of Texas (1848)

The National Baptist Convention, USA (NBC) (1895/1916), the oldest African American Baptist denomination, gave rise in the 20th century to three new groups:

- The first major split created the National Baptist Convention of America (NBCA) (1915).
- The second group emerging from the NBC was the Progressive National Baptist Convention (PNBC) (1961).
- The National Missionary Baptist Convention of America (NMBC) (1988) came out of the NBCA.

The General Association of Regular Baptist Churches (GARBC) (1932)

The Baptist Bible Fellowship International (1950)

The Cooperative Baptist Fellowship (CBF) emerged from the SBC in 1991 over such issues as women's roles and officially separated in 2002. (The CBF permits women pastors; the SBC does not.)

The Baptist World Alliance (BWA) was established in 1905 to network Baptist churches and denominations around the globe. Today, the Alliance has members in over 130 countries and territories.

HOW DO THEY VIEW SCRIPTURE?

Scripture is inspired and without error, the sole, final, totally trustworthy rule of faith. The standard Protestant canon is accepted. (Mainline churches vary in the extent to which they continue to view Scripture as without error.)

HOW DO THEY VIEW GOD AND SALVATION?

The doctrines of the Trinity and the Incarnation are accepted, though historically, most Baptists have not affirmed or made use of the early creeds. People are saved by grace alone when God imputes to them his gift of righteousness through faith alone (*sola fide*) in Christ, who died for their sins. Good works are the inevitable result of true faith but in no way the basis of right standing before God.

WHAT DO THEY BELIEVE HAPPENS AFTER DEATH?

The souls of believers go to be with Christ, and at Christ's return, their bodies are raised to immortal eternal life. The wicked will suffer eternal punishment in hell.

HOW DO THEY VIEW THE CHURCH?

The church (universal) is the body of Christ, which consists of the redeemed throughout history. Local churches are autonomous congregations, and the term *church* usually refers to local congregations.

Members are to be baptized believers. Church officers are pastors and deacons. Churches (congregations) are autonomous but may form associations or conventions for cooperative purposes, especially for evangelism, missions, and education, which are major emphases.

WHAT ABOUT THE SACRAMENTS?

Baptism and the Lord's Supper (Communion) are called ordinances rather than sacraments.

Baptism is immersion of believers only as a symbol of their faith in Christ.

The Lord's Supper is a symbolic memorial of Christ's death and anticipation of his return.

WHAT OTHER THINGS SHOULD WE KNOW?

Separation of church and state is a historic Baptist emphasis, something Baptists affirmed long before most other denominations.

Baptist denominations include both Calvinists and Arminians. Calvinist Baptists are called Particular Baptists, and they adhere to Reformed views of salvation. Arminian Baptists are called General Baptists, and they hold views on salvation similar to Wesleyans or Methodists.

FAMOUS BAPTISTS

- William Carey (1761–1834), "the father of modern missions" and an early leader in the formation of the Baptist Missionary Society (today called the BMS World Mission)
- Charles Spurgeon (1834–1892), a Reformed Baptist pastor in England whose sermons are still popular
- Lottie Moon (1840–1912), a Southern Baptist missionary to China
- Mahalia Jackson (1911–1972), a member of the NBC, one of the most influential gospel singers, steadfastly devoting her singing to gospel music and eventually popularizing it outside African American culture (despite experiencing poverty and discrimination for many years)

- Billy Graham (1918–2018), a Southern Baptist minister and evangelist who preached to more than 200 million people in stadiums and similar venues and to uncounted millions more through television, prompting a reported 3 million people to confess Christ as Savior

- Martin Luther King Jr. (1929–1968), a Baptist minister and the most prominent leader of the civil rights movement in the US

- Charles ("Chuck") Colson (1931–2012), who had converted to Christ shortly before going to prison for his role in the Nixon Watergate scandal, founded Prison Fellowship International; he was a Southern Baptist.

- Jerry Falwell (1933–2007), a controversial Southern Baptist pastor and founder of Liberty University and the Moral Majority in the 1970s

- US presidents: Warren G. Harding (liberal, non-devout Baptist), Harry S. Truman (unorthodox but earnest Baptist), Jimmy Carter (Southern Baptist until after his term of office), and William ("Bill") Clinton (Southern Baptist who left to join the United Methodists with Hillary Clinton at the beginning of his term). In 2007, Carter and Clinton helped form the New Baptist Covenant, a socially and politically progressive network of Baptist congregations.

METHODIST CHURCHES

WHEN AND HOW WERE THEY FOUNDED?

Brothers John and Charles Wesley were devout Anglican ministers. In 1738, after returning to England from

America where they had served as missionaries, both brothers had dramatic experiences of coming to personal faith in Jesus Christ, just three days apart. Their conversion and their ministry that followed were key elements in the Evangelical Revival in Britain, which happened around the same time as the First Great Awakening in America. Adherents of the Wesleys' views were nicknamed Methodists after their methodical way of doing spiritual practices.

In 1784, Methodists in the US, led especially by itinerant preacher Francis Asbury, formed a separate church body. In 1797, a few years after John Wesley's death, the Methodists completed their break from Anglicanism after failed attempts at reconciliation.

HOW MANY ADHERENTS?

- 80 million worldwide
- 12 million or more in the US

WHAT ARE THEIR MAJOR DIVISIONS OR GROUPS?

The United Methodist Church (UMC) (1784), a mainline denomination, took its modern form in 1968 through a merger of some Methodist and Brethren churches. In 2020, the UMC had about 6 million members in the US and 11–12 million worldwide.

John Wesley (1703–1791)

The African Methodist Episcopal Church (AME) (1816), the first Black Protestant denomination in the US, was founded by Richard Allen.

The Wesleyan Church (1843) was founded in the US by abolitionist Methodists.

The Free Methodist Church was founded in 1860. "Free" refers to both its antislavery position and its advocacy of informal worship. Today, it has about 1.6 million members, mostly outside the US.

The Salvation Army (1865 England; 1885 US) was founded by William Booth (a former Methodist minister) and his wife Catherine Booth. Headquartered in London, The Salvation Army reports about 1.65 million members.

The Church of the Nazarene was founded as a single church in Los Angeles in 1895. The denomination now has over 2.6 million members worldwide.

The Global Methodist Church (GMC) was formed in 2022 for conservatives leaving the UMC. Due to the UMC's developing liberal views on sexuality and other issues, roughly a quarter of its churches left for more conservative denominations. In 2024, the GMC reports to have over 4,000 congregations.

HOW DO THEY VIEW SCRIPTURE?

Scripture is inspired and infallible, the sole, final rule of faith. The Protestant canon is accepted.

HOW DO THEY VIEW GOD AND SALVATION?

The doctrines of the Trinity and the Incarnation as taught in the creeds are accepted. People are saved by grace alone when God regenerates and forgives them through faith in Christ, who died for their sins. Good works are the necessary result of true faith, not the means of obtaining forgiveness or salvation.

WHAT DO THEY BELIEVE HAPPENS AFTER DEATH?

The souls of believers go immediately to be with Christ, and at Christ's return, their bodies are raised to immortal, eternal life. The wicked suffer eternal punishment in hell.

HOW DO THEY VIEW THE CHURCH?

The church is the body of Christ, represented by visible church institutions.

Bishops oversee regions and appoint pastors. Methodists do not hold to a strict apostolic succession of bishops but view bishops as elders consecrated to their office.

WHAT ABOUT THE SACRAMENTS?

Baptism is a sign of regeneration and of the new covenant, for adults and children. In the Lord's Supper, Christ is really present and his body and blood spiritually present to believers.

WHAT OTHER THINGS SHOULD WE KNOW?

Methodists teach that "entire sanctification" is a work of the Spirit subsequent to regeneration by which fully consecrated believers are purified of all sin and fit for service, a state maintained by faith and obedience.

Methodists are Arminian; they disagree with the five points of Calvinism.

The Salvation Army and the Church of the Nazarene are often considered Holiness churches because of their ties to the Holiness movement in the 1800s.

The Salvation Army does not practice baptism or the Lord's Supper, preferring to focus on inward spiritual change rather than outward rites.

FAMOUS METHODISTS

- Fanny Crosby (1820–1915), blind from infancy, a composer of over 8,000 hymns, including "Blessed Assurance" and "To God Be the Glory"
- Harriet Tubman (1822–1913), a devout Christian in the AME, who, after escaping slavery, helped dozens of slaves reach freedom through the Underground Railroad and served the Union with remarkable distinction during the Civil War
- George Washington Carver (1864–1943), a premier botanist and committed Christian (in the AME for many years) who viewed his faith as integral with science; he developed the practice of crop rotation and made other advances in agricultural science.
- Jackie Robinson (1919–1972), a strong Methodist Christian who broke the "color line" in US major league baseball
- Rosa Parks (1913–2005), a lifelong member of the AME, famous for her role in the Montgomery Bus Boycott and the civil rights movement
- US presidents: William McKinley (devout, evangelical-minded Methodist), George W. Bush (United Methodist, well-known for his evangelical faith), and James K. Polk (baptized Methodist on his deathbed); Rutherford B. Hayes and Ulysses S. Grant attended Methodist churches, though neither were devout.

HOLINESS MOVEMENT

The Holiness movement grew out of—or some might say, in conjunction with—Methodism. John and Charles Wesley's first Christian gathering was called a "holiness club." But in the century that followed the Wesley brothers, some groups within Methodism believed that the Methodists had lost their first love and forsaken their commitment to entire sanctification (or Christian perfectionism) that the Wesleys had stressed. These groups were known for their emphasis on personal holiness as essential to Christian life, and many broke off from Methodism in the mid to late 1800s.

Phoebe Palmer (1807–1874), an evangelist in New York, was one of the most influential teachers in the Holiness movement. A. B. Simpson (1843–1919), a Canadian-born minister serving in New York, founded what is today called the Alliance World Fellowship, known in the US as the Christian and Missionary Alliance. With roots in the Holiness movement, this denomination differs from Holiness and Methodist churches in that it does not accept the Methodist view of salvation.

The Holiness movement in the 19th century laid the foundation for a major Christian movement that began in the early 20th century: Pentecostalism.

CHURCHES OF CHRIST

WHEN AND HOW WERE THEY FOUNDED?

In 1801, Barton Stone, a Presbyterian pastor in Cane Ridge, Kentucky, held the first interdenominational "camp meeting," with Baptists and Methodists joining the revival. The Cane Ridge Revival became a model for the Second Great Awakening, which lasted into the 1840s.

Barton Stone (1772–1844)

Stone and other Presbyterians in 1804 renounced their ties to the Presbyterians and declared themselves to be simply "Christians." People from various denominations joined this Restoration Movement, so called because it sought to restore a simpler Christianity based in the New Testament. They wanted to be known only as the "Christian church" or the "church(es) of Christ," without denominations or creeds.

In 1815, Thomas Campbell and his son Alexander Campbell began leading a Baptist restoration movement in the Midwest and the South, which later separated from the Baptists. In 1832, many of Stone's "Christians" united with the Campbells' "Disciples of Christ."

HOW MANY ADHERENTS?

- 5–6 million worldwide, especially in Africa and India
- 3 million in the US

WHAT ARE THEIR MAJOR DIVISIONS OR GROUPS?

The Disciples of Christ (Christian Church) is a mainline church (1849/1968).

The Churches of Christ (1906) is a conservative group emphasizing non-instrumental music.

Conservatives in the Disciples of Christ held the first North American Christian Convention, which led to a distinct movement of independent Christian Churches and Churches of Christ (1927).

HOW DO THEY VIEW SCRIPTURE?

"Where the Scriptures speak, we speak; where the Scriptures are silent, we are silent." Scripture is the inerrant word of God. The Protestant canon is accepted.

HOW DO THEY VIEW GOD AND SALVATION?

The creeds are rejected ("no creed but Christ"), but most conservatives accept the ideas of the Trinity and Incarnation. A person must hear the gospel, believe in

Christ, repent, confess Christ, be baptized, and persevere in holiness to be saved. Some groups imply that only people who do this in the Churches of Christ are saved.

WHAT DO THEY BELIEVE HAPPENS AFTER DEATH?

Believers immediately go to be with Christ and at his return are raised to immortality. The wicked suffer eternally in hell.

HOW DO THEY VIEW THE CHURCH?

The church is the assembly of those who have responded rightly to the gospel, and it must be called only by the name of Christ. The most conservative groups maintain that only such churches are part of the restoration of true Christianity. Each local church is autonomous and calls its own pastors.

WHAT ABOUT THE SACRAMENTS?

Baptism is immersion of believers only as the initial act of obedience to the gospel. Many groups recognize only their baptism as valid and believe that baptism is necessary for salvation.

The Lord's Supper is a symbolic memorial.

WHAT OTHER THINGS SHOULD WE KNOW?

Traditionally, they reject denominational labels and centralized church authority.

Most conservative Churches of Christ forbid the use of instrumental music in worship.

FAMOUS CHURCHES OF CHRIST MEMBERS

- Byron Nelson (1912–2006), one of the best golfers in history
- Pat Boone, a popular singer in the 1950s and 1960s and staunch conservative Christian
- Phil Robertson (1946–2025), a star of the TV program *Duck Dynasty*
- Max Lucado, a pastor and bestselling author
- US presidents: James A. Garfield, a devout member of the Church of Christ (he was the only president to have been a former preacher), and Lyndon B. Johnson, a member of the Christian Church (Disciples of Christ)

PENTECOSTAL CHURCHES

WHEN AND HOW WERE THEY FOUNDED?

The term *Pentecostal* refers to Christian groups that seek the same work of the Holy Spirit (resulting in speaking in tongues) that was experienced by the apostles on the day of Pentecost (Acts 2).

In 1901, students at Kansas Bible School led by Charles Fox Parham, a Holiness preacher, began to speak in tongues. A few years later, in 1906, the Azusa Street revival in Los Angeles, led by William Seymour, an African American Holiness preacher, launched Pentecostalism as a movement.

William Seymour (1870–1922)

Some Holiness churches of the late 1800s had proto-Pentecostal views—sometimes even using the term *Pentecostal.* These churches fully embraced Pentecostalism during or following the Azusa Street revival. For example, the Church of God in Christ, which originated in 1897 in Memphis as a predominantly African American Holiness group, became a Pentecostal denomination after their minister, C. H. Mason, participated in the Azusa Street revival.

The first major denomination to originate from within Pentecostalism in the 20th century is the Assemblies of God, founded in 1914.

HOW MANY ADHERENTS?

- 100 million or more worldwide (figures vary widely)
- Roughly 10 million in the US

WHAT ARE THEIR MAJOR DIVISIONS OR GROUPS?

The Church of God in Christ and the Assemblies of God, the largest Pentecostal bodies in the US, each with around 3 million members in the US

The Church of God (Cleveland, TN), with an estimated 1 million members in the US and over 9 million worldwide

The International Church of the Foursquare Gospel (Foursquare Church), founded in 1923 by Aimee Semple McPherson, now with 9 million members worldwide

The International Pentecostal Holiness Church (1911), with 1.5 million members worldwide

In 1989, more than 170 Pentecostal regional denominations formed the World Assemblies of God Fellowship (WAGF). In 2024, the WAGF reported 86 million adherents worldwide, making it the largest Protestant denomination in the world.

HOW DO THEY VIEW SCRIPTURE?

Scripture is inspired and without error, the final, totally trustworthy rule of faith. The Protestant canon is accepted.

HOW DO THEY VIEW GOD AND SALVATION?

The doctrines of the Trinity and the Incarnation are accepted. (Oneness Pentecostals reject the Trinity.) Historically, Pentecostals have not affirmed or made use of the early creeds. Pentecostals teach that people are saved by God's grace, by Christ's death for their sins, through repentance and faith in Christ alone, resulting in being born again to new life in the Spirit, evidenced by a life of holiness.

WHAT DO THEY BELIEVE HAPPENS AFTER DEATH?

The souls of believers go immediately to be with Christ, and at Christ's return, their bodies are raised to immortal, eternal life. The wicked suffer eternal punishment in hell.

HOW DO THEY VIEW THE CHURCH?

The church is the body of Christ, in which the Holy Spirit dwells, which meets to worship God and is the agency for bringing the gospel of salvation to the whole world.

Most Pentecostals practice church government similar to Baptists. Some church bodies view certain leaders as prophets with authoritative messages that are to be confirmed from Scripture.

Pentecostals commonly believe that the church should experience all the spiritual gifts in the New Testament, especially healings, prophecies, and other miracles.

WHAT ABOUT THE SACRAMENTS?

Sacraments are called ordinances.

Baptism is immersion of believers only as an expression of their faith.

The Lord's Supper is a symbolic memorial of Christ's death and anticipation of his return.

WHAT OTHER THINGS SHOULD WE KNOW?

Pentecostals typically view speaking in tongues as the initial evidence of baptism in the Spirit—the second work of grace; salvation, or being "born again," is the first. Charismatics accept speaking in tongues but do not view it as the only initial evidence.

Pentecostal denominations usually hold conservative views on sexuality and oppose same-sex marriage. On women's ordination, there are more diverse practices: the Church of God in Christ does not ordain women as pastors or elders; the Church of God (Cleveland, TN) ordains women as ministers but not as bishops; and the Assemblies of God ordains women to all levels of leadership.

CHARISMATIC AND PENTECOSTALS

The word *charismatic* is often used to describe churches and Christians who practice what are called the charismatic gifts of the Holy Spirit—specifically miracles, healings, prophecy, and speaking in and interpreting tongues. In this sense, Pentecostal churches are *charismatic*, but there are many charismatic churches that differ from the historical Pentecostal denominations. One key difference is that charismatic churches usually do not view tongues as the initial evidence of having received the baptism in the Holy Spirit, as most Pentecostals do.

While prominent Pentecostal denominations emerged from the Azusa Street revival in the early 20th century, many charismatic churches came out of movements in the second half of the 20th century.

- Calvary Chapel began in 1968 in a former Foursquare Gospel church in California pastored by Chuck Smith, a leader in the "Jesus Movement." Calvary Chapel Association now has 1,800 congregations throughout the world.
- The Association of Vineyard Churches was led by former Calvary Chapel pastor John Wimber, famed for teaching modern "signs and wonders" in the 1970s. The Vineyard network now includes over 2,400 churches worldwide.

- The Word of Faith movement, which preaches healing and prosperity as the rights of all Christians, has Assemblies of God roots. Its founder, Kenneth E. Hagin, pastored several Assemblies of God churches before establishing the Kenneth E. Hagin Evangelistic Association in 1963. In 1979, Hagin founded the International Convention of Faith Ministries, which includes nearly 200 churches in the US. The movement has a huge following due to its television programming, especially through the Trinity Broadcasting Network (TBN), founded by Paul Crouch.

Combining Pentecostals, charismatics, and similar groups, researchers estimate there are 500–650 million adherents worldwide, including 10–20 million in the US. These numbers include Oneness churches (which have millions of members), some congregations loosely called Pentecostal, and church movements in nations where statistics are of uncertain reliability. Even with such caveats, this is now easily the second largest church movement, with Catholicism being about twice as large.

FAMOUS PENTECOSTALS AND CHARISMATICS

- Oral Roberts (1918–2009), a Pentecostal who joined the United Methodist Church and a forerunner of the charismatic and Word of Faith movements
- David Yonggi Cho (1936–2021), a Word of Faith advocate who founded Yoido Full Gospel Church in Seoul, South Korea, reportedly the largest church in the world with some 800,000 members (almost 500,000 in Seoul itself)
- T. D. Jakes, a Pentecostal minister, popular speaker, bestselling author, and founder of the Potter's House in Dallas, Texas, a nondenominational megachurch with 30,000 members
- Denzel Washington, a popular actor, outspoken Christian, and the son of a Church of God in Christ pastor
- Juanita Bynum, a Pentecostal evangelist, author, and gospel singer
- Sarah Palin, the former governor of Alaska and Republican candidate for Vice President, member of the Assemblies of God
- Joel Osteen, the pastor of Lakewood Church in Texas, a charismatic megachurch with 45,000 attendees

CURRENT DIVISIONS AND TRENDS

Today, the sharpest division in Christianity is between liberals (or progressives) and evangelicals (or conservatives)—more so than denominational differences. For example, the differences between liberal Methodists and evangelical Methodists are much more significant than those between Methodists and Baptists.

- Liberals view Scripture as fallible and may question whether events such as the virgin birth or the resurrection were literal, historical events. Progressives typically go further, questioning the concept of God as the personal Creator and Ruler of all, and they reject traditional Christian teachings about sexuality and gender.
- Evangelicals generally view Scripture as infallible or inerrant, accepting all of its historical narratives as factual, and they typically hold traditional Christian views about sexuality and gender.

MAINLINE CHURCHES

Some Protestant denominations that originated in the US, mostly in the late 18th and early 19th centuries, became increasingly liberal in theology and practice. Conservative churches often separated from these mainline denominations to form new denominations.

Several mainline denominations attained their current forms and names through mergers in the 20th century.

Mainline denominations generally support progressive views on sexuality and gender, or at least allow their churches and ministers to do so. Liberals or progressives often focus on social liberation over spiritual salvation. Most members believe that souls (at least the souls of believers, and perhaps that of most or all people) go to heaven when they die.

Mainline denominations in the US include:

- United Methodist Church
- Episcopal Church
- Presbyterian Church USA
- American Baptist Churches USA
- Evangelical Lutheran Church in America
- United Church of Christ
- Reformed Church in America
- Christian Church (Disciples of Christ)

Mainline churches in the US have lost roughly a third of their membership, including thousands of congregations, in the 21st century.

HISTORICALLY BLACK CHURCHES

Many historically Black denominations originated as Methodist or Baptist churches, founded by African Americans prior to the Civil War and during Reconstruction. As with mainline churches, these denominations have trended liberal/progressive today. These denominations include:

- African Methodist Episcopal
- African Methodist Episcopal Zion
- Christian Methodist Episcopal
- National Baptist Convention, USA

In the 20th century, the Progressive National Baptist Convention, which broke from the National Baptists, was founded in 1961 to advance the work of Martin Luther King Jr. and the civil rights movement.

Historically Black denominations that are conservative include:

- National Baptist Convention of America
- National Missionary Baptist Convention
- Church of God in Christ

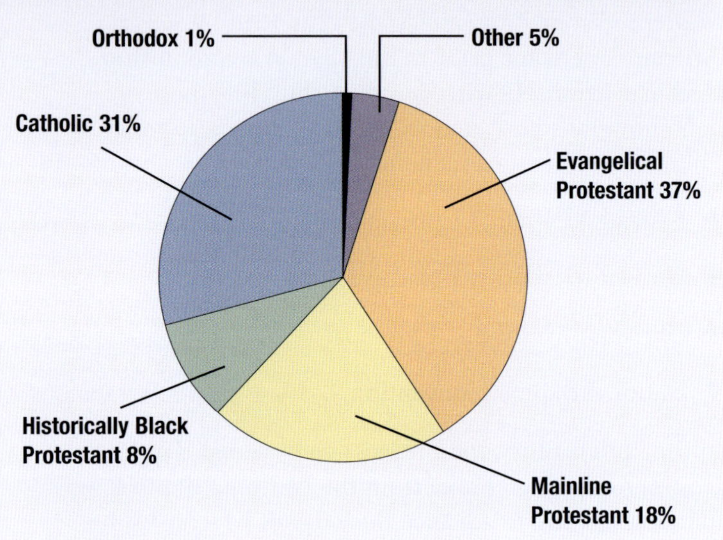

NON-DENOMINATIONAL CHURCHES

The fastest growing segment of Christianity is that of nondenominational churches. It is estimated that nondenominational churches are home to more than 21 million people in the US (where this growing trend appears to be centered). Churches with no formal ties to any denomination have existed for at least a couple centuries, but the number of such congregations has grown dramatically over the past 50 years. There are now more nondenominational church members in the US than Southern Baptists (the largest Protestant denomination). Some of the largest megachurches in the US are nondenominational, frequently forming multisite churches with campuses in different locations in the same city or in nearby towns. In fact, 10 of the 15 largest churches in the US are nondenominational.[4]

Many nondenominational churches broke off from mainline or evangelical denominations, but others were founded as nondenominational from the start. Most of the largest nondenominational churches are evangelical, accepting the Protestant canon as inspired, inerrant Scripture, as well as the doctrines of the Trinity and Incarnation in line with the historic Christian creeds (even if the creeds are not used). All nondenominational churches are by definition congregational, that is, each congregation is autonomous. They also tend to be non-liturgical and less formal in church services. They practice baptism and the Lord's Supper as ordinances, similar to many evangelical Protestant denominations.

ECUMENICAL ORGANIZATIONS

At the start of the 20th century, there was much optimism and a growing interest in bridging denominational divides to foster cooperation among churches. This has been called the ecumenical movement. (The word *ecumenism* comes from Greek words meaning "the whole inhabited world.") Many of the interdenominational organizations that exist today grew out of this movement.

The National Council of the Churches of Christ in the USA, more commonly called the National Council of Churches (NCC), traces its beginnings to 1908 in Philadelphia. It was formed through mergers with other organizations in 1950. Today, the NCC's member denominations include most Orthodox, mainline, and African American church bodies in the US. At one time reaching a peak of 50 million members, the NCC's numbers have declined to about 30 million, reflecting the general decline among mainline denominations. The NCC is part of the larger World Council of Churches.

The World Council of Churches (WCC) was formally organized at its first Assembly in Amsterdam in 1948. Its members today include 352 church bodies in 120 nations representing over 580 million people. The WCC includes Protestant and Orthodox churches, but not the Roman Catholic Church.

In 1912, the World's Evangelical Alliance (originally founded in 1846 as the Evangelical Alliance) was formally incorporated in England. Then, in 1951, evangelical leaders from 21 nations met together and reconstituted the organization, renaming it the World Evangelical Fellowship, with the name changing once again in 2001 to the World Evangelical Alliance (WEA). Today, the WEA includes 143 national alliances of churches totaling more than 600 million people.

One of the national alliances within the WEA is the National Association of Evangelicals (NAE), founded in 1942 in the US. The NAE was established to be a middle way between fundamentalism and progressivism. Today, NAE member denominations include some 45,000 congregations with perhaps as many as 15 million people (many of these denominations do not keep membership numbers). However, many evangelical denominations in the US, including the Southern Baptist Convention and most other Baptist groups, do not participate in the national alliances like the NAE or in the WEA.

HELPFUL WORDS TO KNOW

Anabaptist: Literally, "one who is baptized again." (1) Generally, groups that baptize believers who were already baptized as infants. Anabaptists deny that they are "rebaptizing," since in their view infant baptism is not valid. (2) Specifically, the Anabaptists of Zurich and the church bodies (for example, Mennonites and the Amish) that trace their heritage to them.

Apocrypha: Books included in the Old Testament by Catholics and Orthodox Christians but not Protestants (for example, 1 and 2 Maccabees, Wisdom of Solomon). Called deuterocanonical by those who include them.

apostolic succession: The teaching that church bishops represent an uninterrupted line which traces back to the New Testament apostles. Accepted by Catholic, Orthodox, and Anglican churches.

Arminian: In the theological tradition of Dutch theologian Jacob Arminius (1560–1609), who broke with Calvinists over their beliefs about predestination. Protestants who reject Calvinist doctrines can be considered Arminian, especially most Methodists, Churches of Christ, and Pentecostals.

baptism: A sacrament (or ordinance) of the church in which water is used to sprinkle, pour, or immerse a child or adult. Some denominations only baptize older children or adults who profess a personal faith in Christ (believer's baptism), while others also baptize babies (infant baptism) as a means for their salvation and/or to represent their participation in the covenant community.

Baptist: (1) Anyone who believes that only individuals giving a credible profession of faith should be baptized. (2) Capitalized. A church tradition originating in Puritan England that was congregational and baptist.

Calvinist: In the theological tradition of John Calvin (1509–1564), particularly in Reformed and Presbyterian church bodies, but also some Baptists. Generally, this term can refer to any Protestant who holds to the Calvinist view of predestination and related doctrines of salvation.

canon: Authoritative list of books belonging in the Bible. The Protestant canon has 39 Old Testament books and 27 New Testament books.

catholic: Literally, "universal." (1) The faithful church in all its expressions worldwide. (2) Capitalized. Having to do with the church body headed by the pope—the (Roman) Catholic Church.

charismatic: (1) A generic term for spiritual enabling, as in charismatic gifts (tongues, healings, prophecies, etc.). (2) Church bodies or Christians who practice speaking in tongues and other charismatic gifts but do not view tongues as the initial evidence of having received the baptism in the Holy Spirit. (3) Christians in other denominations who experience charismatic gifts.

confession: (1) A document stating what a particular church body or group of Christians believe in common, such as the Augsburg Confession (Lutheran) and the Westminster Confession of Faith (Presbyterian). (2) The act of privately telling a priest about one's sins. (See *Penance*.)

congregational: (1) A form of church government in which each local church is self-governing; practiced by many denominational groups. (2) Capitalized. A church tradition originating in Puritan England that was congregational in church government but (unlike most others) also accepted infant baptism.

conservative: Retaining the theological position enshrined in the church body's historic creeds or confessions.

creeds: (1) The historic statements of Christian teaching about God (Trinity), Christ, and salvation, including the Nicene Creed (AD 325), the Chalcedonian Creed (AD 451), and others. (2) More generally, statements of doctrine affirmed by a church or group of churches.

dogma: In Catholic teaching, a truth that has been infallibly defined by the church bishops to be divinely revealed; doctrines all members must believe.

Eucharist: Literally, "thanksgiving." Term of choice in liturgical churches for Communion or the Lord's Supper.

evangelical: (1) Conservative Christians, mostly Protestant, who affirm the infallibility or inerrancy of the Bible and view personal conversion (being "born again") as crucial to salvation. (2) Capitalized. Church bodies in the tradition of Martin Luther (1483–1546), whether or not they are evangelical in the general sense—for example, the Evangelical Lutheran Church.

hell: In Christian theology, the final state of the wicked, that is, of the devil, all fallen angels, and all human beings not redeemed by Christ. In the King James Version of the Bible, both the Greek word *Gehenna* (which refers to the final state of the wicked) and the Greek word *Hades* (which refers to the temporary waiting place of all departed human beings between their death and resurrection) are translated as hell.

holiness: (1) God's attribute of sinless perfection, of being beyond and above all impurity or evil—an attribute that human beings are meant to have but do not because of sin. (2) Capitalized. The Christian tradition, stemming from John Wesley, which believes that Christians need a distinct work or effect of God's grace in their lives that makes them personally holy and ready for Christian love and service; or denominations in that tradition (for example, Christian and Missionary Alliance, Nazarenes, and The Salvation Army).

icons: Artworks depicting Jesus, saints, and religious events that are used in worship, mainly in Catholic and Orthodox traditions.

immersion: A form of baptism in which a person is completely submerged under water. Practiced in Baptist churches and in most other churches with a "baptistic" view of the ordinances.

Incarnation: Literally, "in the flesh." The doctrine that Jesus, God the Son, "became flesh" (John 1:14), that is, he became a fully human being while still being also fully God.

inerrant: Without error; used by evangelicals to describe the complete trustworthiness of the Bible in all matters on which it speaks.

infallible: Without error; sometimes understood comprehensively (as in inerrant) and sometimes as limited to certain subjects (especially faith and morals). Applied in Catholicism to the pope to certain pronouncements, and in conservative Catholic and Protestant theology to the Bible.

liberal: Theological views that do not accept the infallibility of the Bible and that question, in varying degrees, the traditional doctrines held in common by most Christians prior to the modern era (such as the virgin birth or the Trinity).

liturgical: A form of corporate worship in which the priest or minister leads the congregation in readings and prayers from a prescribed text called the liturgy.

ordinance: Term of choice in non-liturgical churches for baptism and the Lord's Supper. Regarded as a symbol of God's grace already present in the believer.
(See *sacrament*.)

ordain: To officially appoint someone as a member of the clergy, such as a priest, minister, or pastor of a church or denomination. Ordination is often a formal process that may be accompanied by a religious ceremony, which often includes the laying on of hands (see Acts 6:6; 13:3).

orthodox: (1) Adhering to the essentials of the Christian faith, especially as articulated in the early creeds; in this sense, conservative Catholics, Protestants, and Orthodox are all "orthodox." (2) Capitalized. The association of church bodies of Eastern Europe and the Middle East (Orthodox Church) that are separate from the Catholic Church.

pacifism: Opposition to war, violence, and non-peaceful resistance. Pacifism is especially taught in the Friends, Mennonite, and other "peace church" traditions.

Penance: Catholic sacrament in which a person confesses his or her sins to a priest and is given assurance of forgiveness.

purgatory: A state or place to which believers go after death to have any remaining sin or impurity purged or removed before going to heaven. In the Catholic Church, this is generally regarded as a place of temporal punishment. Most Protestants do not believe in purgatory but rather in an immediate purgation of sin at death.

Puritan: English Protestants who denied that the English monarch was properly the head of the church and who embraced Reformed (Calvinist) theology.

sacrament: Term of choice in liturgical churches for baptism and the Lord's Supper, and for Catholics, five other rites. Regarded in some way as a means for receiving God's grace. (See *ordinance*.)

sanctification: Can refer to an act of God in which a person is declared holy upon belief in Christ and/or the process by which a believer grows spiritually mature in love, righteousness, and holiness. Stressed especially in Methodist and other Holiness traditions.

tongues: Gift of the Spirit in which a person miraculously speaks in a language he or she did not learn or in a "divine" language in prayer. In Pentecostal tradition, speaking in tongues is the sign of the filling (or baptism) in the Holy Spirit.

Trinity: The doctrine that the Father, Son, and Holy Spirit are distinct persons yet by nature fully and equally God.

RESOURCES FOR FURTHER STUDY

BOOKS

Across the Spectrum: Understanding Issues in Evangelical Theology, 3rd ed. by Gregory A. Boyd and Paul Rhodes Eddy (Baker Academic, 2022).

Catechism of the Catholic Church, 2nd ed. (United States Catholic Conference, 2000). Also available at vatican.va.

Christian History Made Easy by Timothy Paul Jones (Rose Publishing, 2009).

Eastern Orthodox Christianity: A Western Perspective, 2nd ed. by Daniel B. Clendenin (Baker Academic, 2003).

Global Christianity: A Guide to the World's Largest Religion from Afghanistan to Zimbabwe by Gina A. Zurlo (Zondervan Academic, 2002).

Handbook of Denominations in the United States, 14th ed. by Roger E. Olson with Craig D. Atwood, Frank S. Mead, and Samuel S. Hill (Abingdon Press, 2018).

Journeys of Faith: Evangelicalism, Eastern Orthodoxy, Catholicism, and Anglicanism by Robert L. Plummer, gen. ed. (Zondervan, 2012).

Roman Catholic Theology and Practice: An Evangelical Assessment by Gregg R. Allison (Crossway, 2014).

Rose Deluxe Timelines: Bible and Christian History (Rose Publishing, 2023)

The Complete Guide to Christian Denominations: Understanding the History, Beliefs, and Differences by Ron Rhodes (Harvest House Publishers, 2015).

The New International Dictionary of Pentecostal and Charismatic Movements. Revised and expanded edition by Stanley M. Burgess and Eduard M. Van der Mass, eds. (Zondervan, 2002).

The Orthodox Church: An Introduction to Eastern Christianity New edition by Timothy Ware (Penguin Books, 2015).

What It Means to Be Protestant: The Case for an Always-Reforming Church by Gavin Ortlund (Zondervan Reflective, 2024).

Why We Belong: Evangelical Unity and Denominational Diversity Anthony L. Chute, Christopher W. Morgan, and Robert A. Peterson, eds. (Crossway, 2013).

WEBSITES

The Association of Religion Data Archives, a source for statistical information. thearda.com

Graphs about Religion by Ryan Burge, data on American religious and Christian trends and beliefs. graphsaboutreligion.com

The Outreach 100 Fastest-Growing and Largest Churches study. outreach100.com

Ready to Harvest, short explainer videos on denominations, their doctrines, and practices. youtube.com/@ReadyToHarvest

Religious Landscape Study. pewresearch.org/religious-landscape-study

NOTES

1 "The 2024 Outreach 100 Fastest-Growing and Largest Churches Study," *Outreach* magazine, Lifeway Research, and the Hartford Institute for Religion Research (2024).

2 "The 2024 Outreach 100 Fastest-Growing and Largest Churches Study."

3 Pie chart developed from data in the "U.S. Religious Landscape Study," Pew Research Center (2023–2024).

4 "The 2024 Outreach 100 Fastest-Growing and Largest Churches Study."

MADE EASY

by Rose Publishing

BIBLE STUDY MADE EASY

HOW WE GOT THE BIBLE MADE EASY

UNDERSTANDING THE HOLY SPIRIT MADE EASY

BIBLE CHRONOLOGY MADE EASY

THE BOOKS OF THE BIBLE MADE EASY

KNOWING GOD'S WILL MADE EASY

WORLD RELIGIONS MADE EASY

BASICS OF THE CHRISTIAN FAITH MADE EASY

SHARING YOUR FAITH MADE EASY

BIBLE TRANSLATIONS MADE EASY

BOOK OF REVELATION

WHO'S WHO IN THE BIBLE

SCRIPTURE MEMORY MADE EASY

END TIMES MADE EASY

CHRISTIAN DENOMINATIONS MADE EASY

ATTRIBUTES OF GOD MADE EASY

rose-publishing.com